I0839851

Chronicles of a Literary Nomad:
The Jack London Story

In the bustling city of San Francisco, on January 12, 1876, a boy named John Griffith London was born, destined to later captivate his readers as Jack London. His birthplace was fittingly close to the Pacific Ocean, as the restless spirit of the sea seemed to course through his veins from an early age.

London's early life was marked by poverty and hardships. His father, William Chaney, was an itinerant astrologer, while his mother, Flora Wellman, struggled as a music teacher. The couple never married, and Jack's upbringing was marred by periods of instability and financial difficulties. Eventually, his mother married John London, a Civil War veteran, and Jack took his stepfather's name.

Despite the challenges that clouded his childhood, London exhibited an insatiable hunger for knowledge. A voracious reader, he relied heavily on the public library to satiate his thirst for learning, using books as gateways to far-off lands and adventures beyond the boundaries of his impoverished existence.

During his teenage years, London developed a rebellious streak and an intense thirst for adventure. This inclination led him to briefly engage in oyster pirating in the waters of the San Francisco Bay—an activity that was not only illegal but also fraught with danger. Through this experience, he gained firsthand insight into the unforgiving realities of life on the seas, deepening his understanding of the challenging existence sailors faced.

In 1897, the discovery of gold in the Klondike region of Yukon, Canada, ignited a frenzied gold rush. Eager to find his fortune, the 21-year-old London joined thousands of prospectors journeying north. The harsh and brutal conditions of the Klondike left a profound impact on him, both physically and emotionally. However, his dreams of striking it rich were never realized. Nevertheless, the Klondike experience served as the inspiration for some of his most famous works.

Back in California, London found himself homeless and unemployed. Determined to survive, he embraced the life of a tramp, riding freight trains and living as a hobo. This nomadic lifestyle exposed him to the struggles of the working class and the desperation of those trying to scrape by during difficult times.

Despite the odds stacked against him, Jack London refused to succumb to his fate. He turned to writing as a way out of poverty, drawing inspiration from his real-life experiences and crafting his stories. Upon his return to California in 1898, he found success in getting his works published. The advent of new printing technologies, which led to cheaper production costs, coupled with a boom in demand for short fiction, further propelled his literary success.

Writing Career and His Best Known Works

The Call of the Wild

In 1903, Jack London's literary breakthrough came with the publication of his most celebrated work, "The Call of the Wild." Set against the backdrop of the Klondike Gold Rush, the novel delves into the profound human-animal connection and explores the dormant primal instincts within every living being.

The story follows Buck, a spirited St. Bernard-Scotch Collie mix, who experiences a dramatic shift from a comfortable domestic life in California to the harsh Klondike wilderness, where he must adapt to the demands of the sled dog life. Through his journey, Buck undergoes a remarkable transformation, shedding the veneer of domestication and embracing his innate instincts for survival. His emotional connection with John Thornton, a kind-hearted prospector, forms the heart of the narrative, leading Buck to face crucial decisions between loyalty to his master and the allure of the untamed wilderness.

The Sea-Wolf

Following the success of "The Call of the Wild," Jack London continued his literary exploration of survival and the complexities of life in his novel "The Sea-Wolf" (1904). "The Sea-Wolf" is a gripping adventure novel that explores themes of power and morality. The story follows Humphrey Van Weyden, a refined literary critic who finds himself shipwrecked after a collision at sea. He is rescued by a seal-hunting schooner, the Ghost, commanded by the enigmatic and brutal Wolf Larsen. As Van Weyden becomes a reluctant member of the crew, he is exposed to a harsh and unforgiving life at sea, contrasting sharply with his life on land.

Larsen, the charismatic and tyrannical captain, embodies a stark contrast to Van Weyden's cultured and intellectual demeanor. The novel delves into the psychological battle between the two men as they clash over principles and authority. Larsen's dominance and disregard for conventional morality challenge Van Weyden's beliefs, leading to a profound transformation in his understanding of life and human nature.

White Fang

Another novel set in the wilderness where untamed spirits roam free, Jack London published his enthralling tale of "White Fang" (1906), a companion novel and a thematic mirror to the acclaimed "The Call of the Wild." This captivating narrative takes a unique approach by presenting the story from the perspective of a wolf-dog named White Fang. Through White Fang's eyes, readers are taken on a journey that delves deep into the complexities of nature versus nurture, revealing the impact of both environment and human influence on the development of an animal's character.

As the narrative unfolds, White Fang experiences a tumultuous life, transitioning from the savage world of the wild to the realm of humans. Captured as a young pup by a Native American tribe, he becomes familiar with the ways of humans and the hardships of domestication. The novel artfully explores the struggles and conflicts within White Fang, as his wild instincts clash with the expectations and demands of the human world. London showcases his remarkable ability to empathize with beings beyond the human sphere, capturing the essence of their thoughts and emotions.

The Iron Heel

As Jack London's reputation as a skilled writer continued to soar, his literary endeavors expanded beyond his gripping tales of adventure. In 1908, he delved into the domain of social-political commentary with the publication of "The Iron Heel," a groundbreaking dystopian novel that would leave a lasting impact on readers.

Set in the distant future, "The Iron Heel" paints a haunting picture of a society dominated by an oppressive oligarchy, known as the "Iron Heel," which holds an iron grip on power and wealth. The story is narrated by Avis Everhard, the wife of revolutionary leader Ernest Everhard, who reflects on the tumultuous events of the past that led to the rise of the oligarchic regime. Through her perspective, readers witness the gradual erosion of democracy and the increasing exploitation of the working class by the ruling elite, culminating in a thought-provoking reflection on the fragility of societal structures and the enduring struggle for justice.

More Stories: South Sea Tales, Martin Eden, John Barleycorn, and The Star Rover

Seeking new inspiration, London and his wife Charmian embarked on a voyage through the South Pacific in 1907. The couple's travels took them to Hawaii, Tahiti, Fiji, and Australia. The lush landscapes, exotic cultures, and encounters with indigenous peoples left a profound impact on London, influencing his later works and deepening his appreciation for the beauty and diversity of the world.

The experiences from their South Pacific journey inspired London to pen a collection of short stories titled "South Sea Tales". These captivating stories, infused with his encounters and observations, transported readers to the enchanting islands of the Pacific, capturing both the allure and the challenges faced by the native islanders.

In 1909, Jack London released "Martin Eden," a semi-autobiographical novel following the struggles of Martin, a working-class sailor aspiring to become a successful writer. The story delves into his relentless pursuit of literary greatness, the challenges of self-education, and the complexities
of fame and success.

The novel stands as a poignant reflection of London's own journey as a budding author, shedding light on the harsh realities of the publishing world. Through Martin Eden's introspective and critically acclaimed narrative, London offers timeless insights into the complexities of artistic ambition and the sacrifices one must make to achieve recognition in the literary sphere.

London's willingness to explore deeply personal and thought-provoking themes is also evident in two more of his notable novels, 'John Barleycorn' (1913) and 'The Star Rover' (1915).

Titled after the personification of alcohol in folk songs, "John Barleycorn," London's autobiographical novel, offered a candid and introspective account of his struggles with alcoholism. Through poignant storytelling, he bared the destructive effects of alcohol on his life, writing career, and relationships, providing a raw and unfiltered examination of the allure and pitfalls of alcohol and the challenges of breaking free from its clutches.

In "The Star Rover," previously known as "The Jacket," London explored the realms of metaphysics and psychology. The novel centered around Darrell Standing, a wrongly convicted prisoner, who, during his time in solitary confinement at San Quentin State Prison, developed the ability to mentally escape his physical surroundings.

Through vivid past-life memories and otherworldly visions, Standing explores the concept of "star-roving," unveiling the potential for greater consciousness and self-discovery. As the boundaries of his confinement blur, Standing's journey becomes a testament to the boundless expanses of the human mind and the enduring quest for inner freedom.

Personal Life and Legacy

In 1897, he married Elizabeth "Bess" Maddern. Although their union was short-lived and ended in 1904, they had two daughters together. London's second marriage to Charmian Kittredge in 1905 proved to be more enduring and provided support throughout his turbulent life. They became inseparable companions in their many travels together. London enjoyed immense commercial success in his writing, striking a chord with readers worldwide, making him one of the highest-paid and most widely read authors of his time.

Despite his success, London battled with alcoholism throughout his life. At the age of 40, Jack London's life came to a tragic end. Struggling with various health issues, including uremia and possible complications from a morphine overdose, he passed away on November 22, 1916. London's untimely death left a void in the literary world, cutting short the career of a prolific and influential writer. However, his legacy as an iconic American author, adventurer, and social advocate endures. His works continue to inspire and captivate readers worldwide.

Jack London's portrayal of the wilderness and the human spirit's resilience resonates across generations, making his stories timeless and deeply heartfelt. London's life was a grand adventure, filled with hardships, triumphs, and an unyielding pursuit of knowledge and understanding. As long as readers aspire to greater horizons, the flame of Jack London's spirit will persist, illuminating a literary legacy that shines brilliantly.

There is an ecstasy
that marks the summit
of life, and beyond
which life cannot rise.
And such is the paradox
of living, this ecstasy
comes when one is most
alive, and it comes as a
complete forgetfulness
that one is alive.

(The Call of the Wild (1903))

A bone to the dog is
not charity. Charity
is the bone shared
with the dog, when
you are just as
hungry as the dog.

("Confession" short story)

I would rather be ashes than
dust! I would rather that my
spark should burn out in a
brilliant blaze than it
should be stifled by dry-rot.
I would rather be a superb
meteor, every atom of me in
magnificent glow, than a
sleepy and permanent planet.
The proper function of man
is to live, not to exist.
I shall not waste my days
in trying to prolong them.
I shall use my time.

(The Bulletin, San Francisco,
California, 1916)

The effect of civilization
is to impose human law upon
environment until it becomes
machine-like in its
regularity. The objectionable
is eliminated, the inevitable
is foreseen. One is not even
made wet by the rain nor cold
by the frost; while death,
instead of stalking about
gruesome and accidental,
becomes a prearranged pageant,
moving along a well-oiled
groove to the family vault,
where the hinges are kept from
rusting and the dust from the
air is swept continually away.

("The Unexpected", Love of Life and
Other Stories)

Man rarely places a
proper valuation upon his
womankind, at least not
until deprived of them.
He has no conception of the
subtle atmosphere exhaled
by the sex feminine, so
long as he bathes in it; but
let it be withdrawn, and an
ever-growing void begins
to manifest itself in his
existence, and he becomes
hungry, in a vague sort of
way, for a something so
indefinite that he cannot
characterize it.

(The Son of the Wolf (1900))

Socialism, when the last word is said, is merely a new economic and political system whereby more men can get food to eat.

(The Human Drift (1917))

There's only one way
to make a beginning,
and that is to begin;
and begin with hard
work, and patience,
prepared for all the
disappointments.

(The Letters of Jack London)

To have a full stomach,
to daze lazily in the
sunshine--such things
were remuneration in full
for his adors and toils,
while his ardors and toils
were in themselves self-
remunerative. They were
expressions of life, and
life is always happy when
it is expressing itself.

(White Fang (1906))

Don't loaf and
invite inspiration;
light out after it
with a club, and if
you don't get it you
will nonetheless
get something that
looks remarkably
like it.

('Getting into Print'
published in The Editor,
1903)

I like the bubbling play of wit, the chesty laughs, the resonant voices of men, when, glass in hand, they shut the grey world outside and prod their brains with the fun and folly of an accelerated pulse.

(John Barleycorn (1913))

In what other land save this
one is the commonest form of
greeting not "Good day," nor
"How d'ye do," but "Love"? That
greeting is Aloha--love,
I love you, my love to you.
Good day--what is it more
than an impersonal remark
about the weather? How do
you do--it is personal in a
merely casual interrogative
sort of a way. But Aloha! It is
a positive affirmation of
the warmth of one's own
heart-giving. My love to
you! I love you! Aloha!

(My Hawaiian Aloha (1916))

You look back and see
how hard you worked
and how poor you were,
and how desperately
anxious you were to
succeed, and all you
can remember is how
happy you were.

(No Mentor but Myself":
Jack London on Writing
and Writers (1979))

A good joke will sell
quicker than a good
poem, and, measured
in sweat and blood,
will bring better
remuneration.

('Getting into Print' published
in The Editor, 1903)

I early learned that there
were two natures in me.
This caused me a great deal
of trouble, till I worked
out a philosophy of life and
struck a compromise between
the flesh and the spirit. Too
great an ascendancy of either
was to be abnormal, and since
normality is almost a fetish
of mine, I finally succeeded
in balancing both natures...
I have small regard for an
utter brute or for an utter
saint.

(The Letters of Jack London)

They were not half
living, or quarter
living. They were
simply so many bags
of bones in which
sparks of life
fluttered faintly.

(The Call of the Wild (1903))

Traditions...bear
heavily upon the
individual,
overmastering his
natural expression
of the love instinct
and forcing him to an
artificial expression
of that love instinct.
He loves, not as his
savage forbears loved,
but as his group loves.

(The Kempton-Wace Letters (1903))

Age is never so old
as youth would
measure it.

('The Wit of Porportuk')

Some sorts of truth
are truer than
others.

(John Barleycorn (1913))

Too much is
written by the men
who can't write
about the men
who do write.

(Martin Eden (1909))

Across Sonoma Mountain wisps of sea fog are stealing. The afternoon sun smoulders in the drowsy sky. I have everything to make me glad I am alive. I am filled with dreams and mysteries. I am all sun and air and sparkle. I am vitalized.

(John Barleycorn (1913))

The pitch to which he was
aroused was tremendous.
All the fighting blood of
his breed was up in him and
surging through him. This was
living, though he did not
know it. He was realizing his
own meaning in the world;
he was doing that for which
he was made.... He was
justifying his existence,
than which life can do no
greater; for life achieves its
summit when it does to the
uttermost that which it was
equipped to do.

(White Fang (1906))

Consider the family
group...such a group becomes
in itself an entity. By means
of the group man is better
enabled to pursue happiness.
But to maintain the group
it must be regulated; so man
formulates rules, codes, dim
ethical laws for the conduct
of the group members.
Sexual ties are made
less promiscuous and more
orderly. A greater privacy
is observed. And out of order
and privacy spring respect
and sacredness.

(The Kempton-Wace Letters (1903))

Love cannot in its very nature be peaceful or content. It is a restlessness, an unsatisfaction. I can grant a lasting love just as I can grant a lasting unsatisfaction; but the lasting love cannot be coupled with possession, for love is pain and desire and possession is easement and fulfilment.

(The Kempton-Wace Letters (1903))

Cruelty, as a fine art,
has attained its
perfect flower in the
trained-animal world.

(Michael, Brother of Jerry (1917))

Go strip off your
clothes that are a
nuisance in this
mellow clime. Get in
and wrestle with the
sea; wing your heels
with the skill and
power that reside
in you, hit the sea's
breakers, master them,
and ride upon their
backs as a king should.

(The Cruise of the Snark (1911))

At first, you fear you
will die; then, after
it has a good hold on
you, you fear you
won't die.

(Of seasickness)

(The Cruise of the Snark (1911))

The Law is a lie, and
through it men lie
most shamelessly.

(The People of the Abyss (1903))

Pray do not
interrupt me...
I am smiling.

(The Sea-Wolf (1904))

Pursuit and possession are accompanied by states of consciousness so wide apart that they can never be united.

(The Kempton-Wace Letters (1903))

Be delicate, little wife-woman.
Never be without your veil, without
many veils. Veil yourself in a
thousand veils, all shimmering and
glittering with costly textures and
precious jewels. Never let the last
veil be drawn. Against the morrow
array yourself with more veils, ever
more veils, veils without end. Yet
the many veils must not seem many.
Each veil must seem the only one
between you and your hungry lover
who will have nothing less than all
of you. Each time he must seem to get
all, to tear aside the last veil that
hides you. He must think so. It must
not be so. Then there will be no
satiety, for on the morrow he will
find another last veil that has
escaped him.

(The Valley of the Moon (1913))

I'd rather sing one
wild song and burst my
heart with it, than
live a thousand years
watching my digestion
and being afraid of
the wet.

(The House of Pride, and Other
Tales of Hawaii (ed. 1919))

A human life the
treasure of the world
cannot buy; nor can it
redeem one which is
misspent; nor can it
make full and complete
and beautiful a life
which is dwarfed and
warped and ugly.

(Tales of the North)

There are roads and
roads, and of truth
there are orders and
orders.

(John Barleycorn (1913))

Fear urged him to go
back, but growth
drove him on.

(White Fang (1906))

Comes the lover, tricked by
nature, blind of passion,
impelled madly toward the
loved one. He is as blind to
her salient imperfections as
he is to her petty vices. He
does not interrogate her
disposition and temperament,
or speculate as to how they
will coordinate with his for
two score years and odd. He
questions nothing, desires
nothing, save to possess her.
And this is the paradox:
By nature he is driven to
contract a temporary tie,
which, by social observance
and demand, must endure
for a lifetime.

(The Kempton-Wace Letters (1903))

Don't write too
much. Concentrate
your sweat on one
story, rather than
dissipate it over a
dozen.

('Getting into Print'
published in The Editor,
1903)

They are fighters.
They love peace. They are
unafraid of war. They intend
nothing less than to destroy
existing capitalist society
and to take possession of the
whole world. If the law of
the land permits, they fight
for this end peaceably,
at the ballot box. If the law
of the land does not permit,
and if they have force meted
out to them, they resort to
force themselves.

(Revolution and Other Essays
(1910))

But I am I.
And I won't
subordinate
my taste to the
unanimous
judgment of
mankind.

(Martin Eden (1909))

Somehow, the love of the islands, like the love of a woman, just happens. One cannot determine in advance to love a particular woman, nor can one so determine to love Hawaii.

(The New Hawaii (1923))

Life, in a sense,
is living and
surviving. And all
that makes for living
and surviving is
good. He who follows
the fact cannot go
astray, while he who
has no reverence for
the fact wanders afar.

(The Kempton-Wace Letters
(1903))

All my life I have had an awareness of other times and places. I have been aware of other persons in me. Oh, and trust me, so have you, my reader that is to be. Read back into your childhood, and this sense of awareness I speak of will be remembered as an experience of childhood. You were then not fixed, not crystallized. You were plastic, a soul in flux, a consciousness and an identity in the process of forming--ay, of forming and forgetting.

(The Star Rover (1915))

Heaven forefend me from the most of
the average run of male humans who
are not good fellows, the ones cold
of heart and cold of head who don't
smoke, drink, or swear, or do much
of anything else that is brase, and
resentful, and stinging, because in
their feeble fibres there has never
been the stir and prod of life to
well over its boundaries and be
devilish and daring. One doesn't
meet these in saloons, nor rallying
to lost causes, nor flaming on the
adventure-paths, nor loving as
God's own mad lovers. They are too
busy keeping their feet dry,
conserving their heart-beats, and
making unlovely life-successes of
their spirit-mediocrity.

(John Barleycorn (1913))

It appears that
in this life of
experience...we pay
just as dearly for
our triumphs as we
do for our defeats.

She was thrilling to a
desire that urged her
to go forward, to be in
closer to that fire,
to be squabbling with
the dogs, and to be
avoiding and dodging
the stumbling feet of
men.

(White Fang (1906))

If cash comes with
fame, come fame; if
cash comes without
fame, come cash.

(The Letters of Jack London)

As one grows weaker
one is less susceptible
to suffering. There is
less hurt because
there is less to hurt.

(The Star Rover (1915))

Love is the sum of all the arts, as it is the reason for their existence.

(The Valley of the Moon (1913))

These women, capable
of the most sublime
emotions, of the
tenderest sympathies,
were openmouthed and
screaming. They
wanted to live, they
were helpless, likes
rats in a trap, and
they screamed.

(The Sea-Wolf (1904))

Man is a flux of states
of consciousness,
a flow of passing
thoughts, each thought
of self another self,
a myriad thoughts,
a myriad selves,
a continual becoming
but never being,
a will-of-the-wisp
flitting of ghosts
in ghostland.

(John Barleycorn (1913))

As for the primitive, I hark
back to it because we are
still very primitive. How
many thousands of years of
culture, think you, have
rubbed and polished at our
raw edges? One probably; at
the best, no more than two.
And that takes us back to
screaming savagery, when,
gross of body and deed, we
drank blood from the skulls
of our enemies, and hailed as
highest paradise the orgies
and carnage of Valhalla.

(The Kempton-Wace Letters (1903))

Man is man because
he chanced to develop
intelligence instead
of instinct; otherwise
he would to this day
have remained among
the anthropoid apes.
He has turned away
from nature, become
unnatural, as it were,
disliked the earth
upon which he found
himself, and changed
the face of it somewhat
to his liking.

(The Kempton-Wace Letters
(1903))

There is another way
of disqualifying the
metaphysicians....
Judge them by their
works. What have they
done for mankind
beyond the spinning
of airy fancies and the
mistaking of their own
shadows for gods?

(The Iron Heel (1907))

There is more than the
germ of truth... in the
child's definition of
memory as the thing one
forgets with. To be able
to forget means sanity.
Incessantly to remember
means obsession, lunacy.

(The Star Rover (1915))

I write for no other
purpose than to add
to the beauty that
now belongs to me.

(Jack London, American rebel
(1947))

But this is not a world of free freights. One pays according to an iron schedule--for every strength the balanced weakness; for every high a corresponding low; for every fictitious god-like moment an equivalent time in reptilian slime. For every feat of telescoping long days and weeks of life into mad magnificent instants, one must pay with shortened life, and, oft-times, with savage usury added.

(John Barleycorn (1913))

The life that is
demanding to be born
is limitless. Nature
is a spendthrift...
For that matter,
look at you and me.
In our loins are the
possibilities of
millions of lives.

(Before Adam (1917))

A million years ago, the cave man, without tools, with small brain, and with nothing but the strength of his body, managed to feed his wife and children, so that through him the race survived. You on the other hand, armed with all the modern means of production, multiplying the productive capacity of the cave man a million times — you are incompetents and muddlers, you are unable to secure to millions even the paltry amount of bread that would sustain their physical life. You have mismanaged the world, and it shall be taken from you.

(Speaking to a group of wealthy New Yorkers during a campaign)

I remembered my days
and nights of sunshine
and starshine, where
life was all a wild
sweet wonder,
a spiritual paradise
of unselfish adventure
and ethical romance.
And I saw before me,
ever blazing and
burning, the Holy
Grail.

(London's Essays of Revolt (ed.
1926))

My life shall be free
and broad and great,
and I will not be the
slave to the sense
delights which
chained my ancient
ancestry. I reject the
heritage. I break the
entail. And who are
you to say I am unwise?

(The Kempton-Wace Letters (1903))

For the pride of trace and trail was his, and sick unto death, he could not bear that another dog should do his work.

(The Call of the Wild (1903))

A scab is a two-legged
animal with a corkscrew
soul, a waterlogged
brain, a combination
backbone of jelly and
glue. Where others have
hearts, he carries a
tumor of rotten
principles.

(Ode to a scab)

Denied the outlet, through play, of his energies, he recoiled upon himself and developed his mental processes. He became cunning; he had idle time in which to devote himself to thoughts of trickery.

(White Fang (1906))

He was sounding the
deeps of his nature,
and of the parts of
his nature that were
deeper than he, going
back into the womb of
Time.

(The Call of the Wild (1903))

I do not live for what
the world thinks of
me, but for what I
think of myself.

(Letter to Charles Warren
Stoddard (1903))

Hawaii is a paradise—
and I can never cease
proclaiming it; but I
must append one word
of qualification:
Hawaii is a paradise
for the well-to-do.

(My Hawaiian Aloha, 1916)

I believe that when
I am dead, I am dead.
I believe that with
my death I am just as
much obliterated as
the last mosquito
you and I squashed.

(The Call of the Wild (1903))

Life creeps slowly upward....
When some forgotten inventor
of the older world smote his
rival or enemy with a branch
of wood and found that it was
good and thereafter made a
practice of smiting rivals
and enemies with branches of
wood, then, and on that day,
artificiality may be said to
have begun. Then, and on that
day, was begun a revolution
destined to change the history
of life. Then, and on that day,
was laid the cornerstone of
that most tremendous of
artifices, CIVILIZATION!

(The Kempton-Wace Letters (1903))

The trouble with him was that he was without imagination. He was quick and alert in the things of life, but only in the things, and not in the significances. Fifty degrees below zero meant eighty-odd degrees of frost. Such fact impressed him as being cold and uncomfortable, and that was all. It did not lead him to meditate upon his frailty as a creature of temperature, and upon man's frailty in general, able only to live within certain narrow limits of heat and cold; and from there on it did not lead him to the conjectural field of immortality and man's place in the universe.

(To Build a Fire (1902))

It was the freshness and the
newness of your beauty and
you, the mystery of you, that
won your man. When a man
has plucked and smelled all
the sweetness of a flower,
he looks for other flowers.
It is his queerness.
You must ever remain a
flower almost plucked yet
never plucked, stored with
vats of sweet unbroached
though ever broached.

(The Valley of the Moon (1913))

He loved to run in the
dim twilight of the
summer midnights,
listening to the
subdued and sleepy
murmurs of the forest,
reading signs and
sounds as a man may
read a book, and
seeking for the
mysterious something
that called...

(The Call of the Wild (1903))

Our ape-like and
arboreal ancestors
entered upon the first of
many short cuts. To crack
a marrow-bone with a
rock was the act which
fathered the tool, and
between the cracking of
a marrow-bone and the
riding down town in an
automobile lies only a
difference of degree.

(The Kempton-Wace Letters (1903))

Be not misled into the belief
that love is finer and higher than
affection and friendship, that the
yielding to its blandishment is
higher wisdom on the part of our
lovers. Not so; they are puppets
and know and think nothing about
it. They come of those who yielded
likewise in the past. They obey
forces beyond them, greater than
they, their kind, and all life,
great as the great forces of the
physical universe. Our lovers are
children of duty, natural and
uninventive. Duty and moral
responsibility are less to them
than passion. They will obey and
procreate though the heavens roll
up as a scroll and all things come
to judgment.

(The Kempton-Wace Letters (1903))

The fortunate man is
the one who cannot
take more than a
couple of drinks
without becoming
intoxicated. The
unfortunate wight is
the one who can take
many glasses without
betraying a sign; who
must take numerous
glasses in order to
get the kick.

(John Barleycorn (1913))

It is so much
easier to live
placidly and
complacently.
Of course, to live
placidly and
complacently is
not to live at all.

(Works of Jack London (1980))

Everything is good...
as long as it is
unpossessed. Satiety
and possession are
Death's horses they
run in span.

(The Cruise of the Snark (1911))

Let us suppose the loved one
is as madly impelled toward
the lover...So great, so
intense is it, that the world
could crumble to star-dust so
long as their souls rushed
together. If necessary, they
would break all ties, forsake
all friends, abandon all
blood kin, run away from
all moral responsibilities.
There can be no discussion.....
We see it every day, for love
is the most perfectly selfish
thing in the universe.

(The Kempton-Wace Letters (1903))

He became quicker of
movement than the other
dogs, swifter of foot,
craftier, deadlier, more
lithe, more lean with
ironlike muscle and sinew,
more enduring, more cruel
more ferocious, and more
intelligent. He had to
become all these things,
else he would not have held
his own nor survived the
hostile environment in
which he found himself.

(White Fang (1906))

Darn the wheel of the world! Why must it continually turn over? Where is the reverse gear?

(Delphi Complete Works of Jack London (Illustrated))

There is such a thing
as anesthesia of pain,
engendered by pain
too exquisite to be
borne.

(The Star Rover (1915))

He lacked the wisdom,
and the only way for
him to get it was to
buy it with his
youth; and when
wisdom was his, youth
would have been spent
buying it.

("A Piece of Steak" from The Best
Short Stories of Jack London
(1962))

The great task demanded of man is reproduction. He is urged by passion to perform this task. Passion, working through the imagination, produces love. Passion is the impelling factor, imagination the disturbing factor; and the disturbance of passion by imagination produces love.

(The Kempton-Wace Letters (1903))

As for me, you wonder
why I am a socialist. I'll
tell you. It is because
socialism is inevitable;
because the present
rotten and irrational
system cannot endure;
because the day is past
for your man on
horseback. The slaves
won't stand for it. They
are too many, and willy-
nilly they'll drag down
the would-be equestrian
before he gets astride.

(Martin Eden (1909))

Men do not knowingly drink for the effect alcohol produces on the body. What they drink for is the brain-effect; and if it must come through the body, so much the worse for the body.

(John Barleycorn (1913))

A vast silence reigned over the land. The land itself was a desolation, lifeless, without movement, so lone and cold that the spirit of it was not even that of sadness. There was a hint in it of laughter, but of laughter more terrible than any sadness-a laughter that was mirthless as the smile of the Sphinx, a laughter cold as the frost and partaking of the grimness of infallibility. It was the masterful and incommunicable wisdom of eternity laughing at the futility of life and the effort of life. It was the Wild.

(White Fang (1906))

One cannot violate the promptings of one's nature without having that nature recoil upon itself.

(White Fang (1906))

Do you know the only value life
has is what life puts upon itself?
And it is of course overestimated,
for it is of necessity prejudiced
in its own favour. Take that man I
had aloft. He held on as if he were
a precious thing, a treasure
beyond diamonds of rubies. To you?
No.
To me? Not at all. To himself? Yes.
But I do not accept his estimate.
He sadly overrates himself. There
is plenty more life demanding to
be born. Had he fallen and dripped
his brains upon the deck like
honey from the comb, there would
have been no loss to the world.
The supply is too large.

(The Sea-Wolf (1904))

A good soldier is a
blind, heartless,
soulless, murderous
machine...All that is
human in him, all that is
divine in him, all that
constitutes the man has
been sworn away when he
took the enlistment roll.
His mind, his conscience,
aye, his very soul, are in
the keeping of his
officer.

(Jack London reports: War
correspondence, sports articles,
and miscellaneous writings
(ed. 1970))

"Then one can't make a
living out of poetry?"

"Certainly not. What
fool expects to? Out
of rhyming, yes."

(Martin Eden (1909))

And how have I lived?
Frankly and openly,
though crudely. I have
not been afraid of life.
I have not shrunk from
it. I have taken it for
what it was at its own
valuation. And I have
not been ashamed of it.
Just as it was, it was
mine.

(The Letters of Jack London)

White Fang knew the law
well: TO OPPRESS THE WEAK
AND OBEY THE STRONG.
He ate his share of meat as
rapidly as he could. And
then woe the dog that had
not yet finished! A snarl
and a flash of fangs, and
that dog would wail
his indignation to the
uncomforting stars while
White Fang finished his
portion for him.

(White Fang (1906))

When, on the still cold
nights, he pointed his nose
at a star and howled long
and wolf-like, it was his
ancestors, dead and dust,
pointing nose at star and
howling down through the
centuries and through him.
And his cadences were their
cadences, the cadences
which voiced their woe
and what to them was the
meaning of the stillness,
and the cold, and dark.

(The Call of the Wild (1903))

Life? Bah! It has no
value. Of cheap things
it is the cheapest.
Everywhere it goes
begging. Nature spills
it out with a lavish
hand. Where there is
room for one life, she
sows a thousand lives,
and it's life eats life
till the strongest and
most piggish life
is left.

(The Sea-Wolf (1904))

The ghostly winter
silence had given
way to the great
spring murmur of
awakening life.

(The Call of the Wild (1903))

He was mastered by the
sheer surging of life,
the tidal wave of being,
the perfect joy of each
separate muscle, joint,
and sinew in that it was
everything that was not
death, that it was aglow
and rampant, expressing
itself in movement,
flying exultantly
under the stars.

(The Call of the Wild (1903))

It is a simple matter to see the
obvious, to do the expected. The
tendency of the individual life is
to be static rather than dynamic,
and this tendency is made into a
propulsion by civilization, where
the obvious only is seen, and the
unexpected rarely happens.
When the unexpected does happen,
however, and when it is of
sufficiently grave import, the
unfit perish. They do not see what
is not obvious, are unable to do
the unexpected, are incapable of
adjusting their well-grooved lives
to other and strange grooves.
In short, when they come to the end
of their own groove, they die.

(The Unexpected (1906))

He was not immoral, but merely unmoral.

(The Sea-Wolf (1904))

Desire is a pain which seeks easement through possession.

(The Kempton-Wace Letters (1903))

With the aurora borealis
flaming coldly overhead,
or the stars leaping in the
frost dance, and the land
numb and frozen under its
pall of snow, this song of the
huskies might have been the
defiance of life, only it was
pitched in minor key, with
long-drawn wailings and
half-sobs, and was more the
pleading of life, the
articulate travail of
existence. It was an old
song, old as the breed
itself--one of the first
songs of the younger world
in a day when songs were sad.

(The Call of the Wild (1903))

Ever bike? Now that's something that makes life worth living!... Oh, to just grip your handlebars and lay down to it, and go ripping and tearing through streets and road, over railroad tracks and bridges, threading crowds, avoiding collisions...and wondering all the time when you're going to smash up. Well, now, that's something! And then go home again after three hours of it... and then to think that tomorrow I can do it all over again!

(The Letters of Jack London)

But, - and there it is,
- we want to live and
move, though we have
no reason to, because
it happens that it is
the nature of life to
live and move, to want
to live and move. If it
were not for this, life
would be dead. It is
because of this life
that is in you that
you dream of your
immortality.

(The Sea-Wolf (1904))

I did not begin when
I was born, nor when
I was conceived. I have
been growing, developing,
through incalculable
myriads of millenniums...
All my previous selves
have their voices, echoes,
promptings in me... Oh,
incalculable times again
shall I be born.

(The Star Rover (1915))

The most beautiful
stories always start
with wreckage.

(To Build a Fire (1902))

Limited minds
can recognize
limitations
only in others.

(Martin Eden (1909))

There are, broadly speaking, two types of drinkers. There is the man whom we all know, stupid, unimaginative, whose brain is bitten numbly by numb maggots; who walks generously with wide-spread, tentative legs, falls frequently in the gutter, and who sees, in the extremity of his ecstasy, blue mice and pink elephants.... The other type of drinker has imagination, vision. Even when most pleasantly jingled he walks straight and naturally, never staggers nor falls, and knows just where he is and what he is doing. It is not his body but his brain that is drunken.

(John Barleycorn (1913))

The human race is
doomed to sink back
farther and farther
into the primitive
night ere again it
begins its bloody
climb upward to
civilization.

(The Call of the Wild (1903))

www.ingramcontent.com/pod-product-compliance
Lightning Source LLC
Chambersburg PA
CBHW012258240726
48656CB00007B/2441